Lives and Times

Asa Candler

The Founder of Coca-Cola®

Rebecca Vickers

Heinemann Library
Chicago, Illinois

Customer Service 888-454-2279
Visit our website at www.heinemannlibrary.com

Designed by Richard Parker and Mike Hogg (Maverick)
Photo research by Jill Birschbach
Printed and bound in China by South China Printing Company Limited

09 08 07 06 05
10 9 8 7 6 5 4 3 2 1

Library of Congress Cataloging-in-Publication Data
Vickers, Rebecca.
    Asa Candler : the man who brought us Coca-Cola / Rebecca Vickers.
        p. cm. -- (Lives and times)
    Includes bibliographical references and index.
    ISBN 1-4034-6343-3 (lib. bdg.) -- ISBN 1-4034-6357-3 (pbk.)
1. Candler, Asa Griggs, 1851-1929--Juvenile literature. 2. Coca-Cola Company--Biography--Juvenile literature. 3. Soft drink industry--United States--Biography--Juvenile literature. 4. Capitalists and financiers--Georgia--Atlanta--Biography--Juvenile literature. I. Title. II. Series: Lives and times (Des Plaines, Ill.)
    HD9349.S632V53 2005
    338.7'66362'092--dc22

                        2004021939

Acknowledgments
The author and publishers are grateful to the following for permission to reproduce copyright material:
pp. p. 4 Kalish/DiMaggio/Corbis; pp. 5, 16 John Van Hasselt/Corbis Sygma; pp. 6, 12, 13, 25 Special Collections Department, Robert W. Woodruff Library, Emory University; pp. 7, 18, 21, 22 Bettmann/Corbis; pp. 8, 24 Corbis; pp. 9, 10, 11, 14, 15, 19 Courtesy, Georgia Archives; pp. 17, 20 The Advertising Archive Ltd.; p. 23 Underwood & Underwood/Corbis; p. 26 Ken Straton/Corbis; p. 27 ChromoSohm Inc./Corbis

Cover photograph by John Van Hasselt/Corbis Sygma

Cover and interior icons Janet Lankford Moran/Heinemann Library

Coca-Cola® is the registered trademark of The Coca-Cola Company

Every effort has been made to contact copyright holders of any material reproduced in this book. Any omissions will be rectified in subsequent printings if notice is given to the publishers.

Some words are shown in bold, **like this**. You can find out what they mean by looking in the glossary.

Contents

A Drink for the World

Soft drinks are sold in cans and bottles all over the world. They come in hundreds of different flavors. The most famous soft drink is Coca-Cola®.

Today The Coca-Cola® **Company** makes many different drinks.

Coca-Cola® was first made about 120 years ago. Then it was made as a drink to make people feel better. Asa Candler started the company that put the drink into bottles and sold it around the world.

Asa Candler's company made the most famous soft drink in the world.

Early Years

Asa Candler was born on December 30, 1851, near Villa Rica, Georgia. Asa's father was an important farmer. His mother took care of their eleven children.

Here is a picture of Asa when he was a young child.

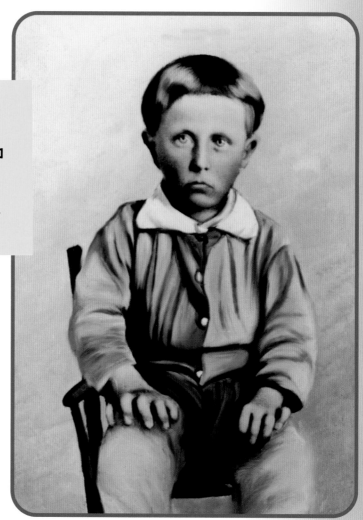

Asa sold his furs in stores like this one.

When Asa was a young boy, he sold furs and bought straight pins with the money he made. Asa then sold the pins to make more money.

A Wartime Childhood

Asa went to school in Villa Rica, Georgia. When he was nine years old, the **Civil War** started. Many fierce battles took place in Georgia.

Atlanta, Georgia was in ruins after the Civil War.

Asa missed a lot of school during the war. He went to high school for only two years. Then he got a job as an **apprentice** in a drugstore in Cartersville, Georgia.

This is Cartersville in Georgia. Asa worked here for a **pharmacist** in a drugstore.

Moving to the City

After nearly three years in Cartersville, Asa got a job in a drugstore in Atlanta. Atlanta was now the **capital** of Georgia.

This is how Atlanta looked in the late 1800s. The city was burned down during the **Civil War**. It had to be rebuilt.

Young men worked in drugstores mixing medicines, working the soda fountains, and helping **customers**.

Dr. George J. Howard owned drugstores in Atlanta. Asa worked in one of them for a while.

A Young Businessman

Asa worked for Dr. Howard for a few years. Then Asa and his friend, Marcellus Hallman, bought one of Dr. Howard's stores.

This is a picture of one of Asa's drugstores in Atlanta.

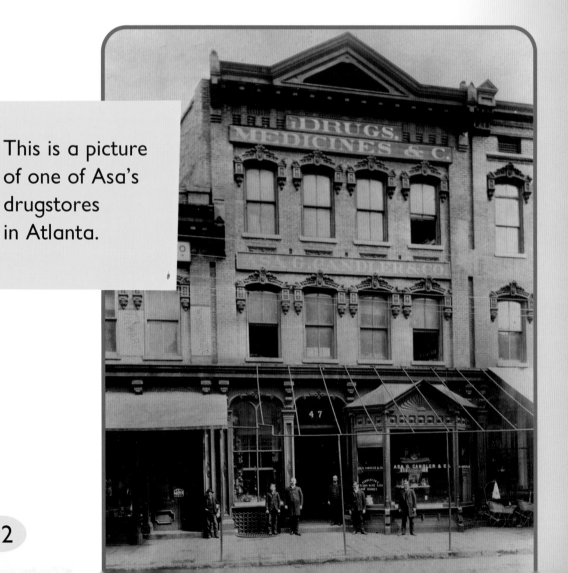

When he was 26 years old, Asa married Dr. Howard's 18-year-old daughter, Lucy. In 1881 Asa bought Marcellus's share of the **business**. He now had his own stores!

This is where Asa and Lucy lived in Atlanta.

Family Life

Asa and Lucy's first son, Charles Howard, was born in December 1878. The next year they bought their first house. Asa was now a successful Atlanta **businessman**. He bought more **businesses**. Most of them made money.

Asa and Lucy had four sons and one daughter.

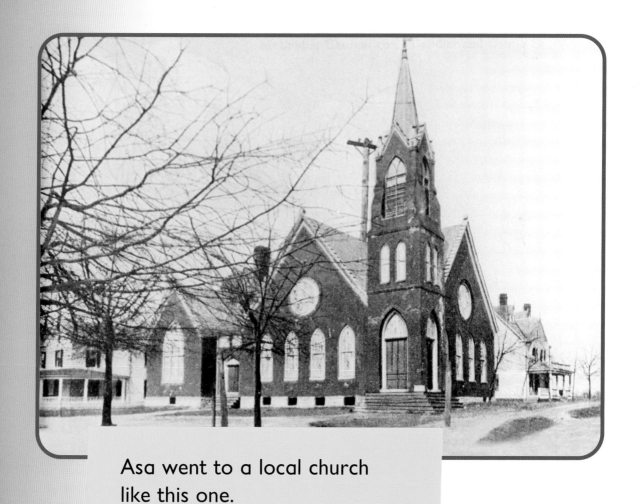

Asa went to a local church
like this one.

Religion was very important to Asa. As
well as being a businessman, he was also
a Sunday school teacher.

Pemberton's Formula

In 1886 an Atlanta **pharmacist** named John S. Pemberton made a **formula** for a new **tonic** drink to make people feel better.

This is a picture of John S. Pemberton. He **invented** many medicines and drinks.

Pemberton's **bookkeeper**, Frank Robinson, named this new drink Coca-Cola®. He wrote the words out in a curly writing style. The new drink was very popular.

Frank Robinson chose the name Coca-Cola® and designed the way to write it.

A New Company

Asa knew about Pemberton and his drinks. He thought that Coca-Cola® could be a success, so he bought Pemberton's **formula**.

This is Marietta Street in Atlanta, Georgia, where Coca-Cola® was first made and put into bottles.

In the early 1900s, Coca-Cola® was delivered in wagons like this one.

Asa wanted Coca-Cola® to be sold to people everywhere. He started The Coca-Cola® **Company**, to make and sell the drink.

Big Business

Asa was right about Coca-Cola®. A lot of people liked it and wanted to buy it. He had to open big **factories** to make as much as he could.

In 1916 the bottle shape on the right was chosen to be the only style of Coca-Cola® bottle.

Asa made sure people knew about his drink by using **advertising**.

Asa wanted people all over the United States to know about Coca-Cola®. He started using salespeople and advertising in magazines and newspapers.

Success and Problems

The Coca-Cola® **Company** was very successful. By 1900 Asa was selling cola across the United States. However, the company did have some problems.

This is an early **advertisement** for Coca-Cola®.

After 1909 Coca-Cola® was sold just as a soft drink—not a **tonic**.

In 1909 the U.S. government said that Coca-Cola® might not be good for people. Asa agreed to make changes. Coca-Cola® was now advertised just as a soft drink, not a tonic or medicine.

Handing Over Control

By 1915 Coca-Cola® was for sale in many places besides Atlanta. In 1917 Asa gave the **company** to his children.

Before **World War I** started, Asa and Lucy went on a long vacation in Europe. This is Paris, France, at that time.

This is Asa and Lucy's house in Atlanta, Georgia. Asa was mayor of Atlanta from 1916 to 1918.

Asa's wife Lucy died in March 1919. In September 1919 the Candler children sold the company. Asa was very unhappy about this. He died in 1929.

More About Asa

Asa Candler made Coca-Cola® a popular drink worldwide. The **company** has continued to grow. Today you can buy Coca-Cola® in almost 200 countries.

Coca-Cola® is now sold all over the world. Here it is being **advertised** in Tokyo, Japan.

People have written books about the story of Asa Candler and his company. There is a Coca-Cola® museum in Atlanta, Georgia.

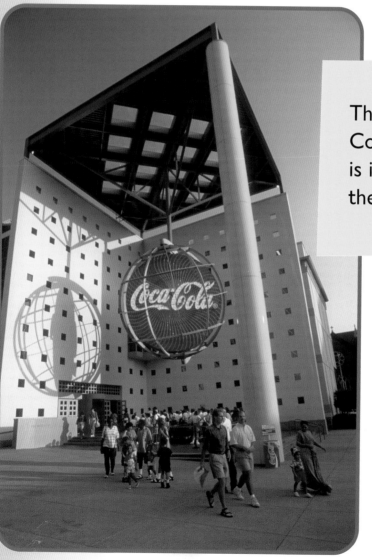

The World of Coca-Cola® Museum is in Atlanta, where the company started.

Fact File

- Sam Candler, Asa's father, named the town of Villa Rica, Georgia. Villa Rica means "rich village."

- Asa Candler was very short. He was just a little over five feet tall. He was known for his high, squeaky voice.

- Asa gave more than $8 million to Emory University. He helped move it from Oxford, Georgia, to Atlanta.

- Santa Claus is usually shown as a chubby, happy person in a red suit with white trim. This is because the Coca-Cola® **advertisements** showed him that way in 1931.

- "Coca-Cola®" is the second most-recognized word in the world. The most-recognized word is "okay."

Timeline

1851	Asa Candler is born on December 30
1870	Asa becomes an **apprentice** at a drugstore in Cartersville, Georgia
1873	Asa moves to Atlanta, Georgia
1878	Asa marries Lucy Howard
1881	Asa sets up Asa Candler and **Company**
1886	John S. Pemberton **invents** the Coca-Cola® **formula**
1887	Asa buys the formula for Coca-Cola®
1892	The Coca-Cola® Company starts
1899	Coca-Cola® is sold in bottles in many places
1917	Asa Candler gives his children the company
1919	Lucy Candler dies. The family sells control of The Coca-Cola® Company
1929	Asa Candler dies

Glossary

advertise/ advertisement show or tell people about something they can buy

apprentice someone who works for a person while learning the job

bookkeeper person who keeps the money records for a company

business trade or activity that earns money

businessman person who works in a business

capital city where state government is based

Civil War war from 1861 to 1865 between the northern states and the southern states

company group of people who makes money by selling things

customers people who buy goods

factory place where things are made

formula method and ingredients to make something

inventing making something that has never been made before

pharmacist someone trained to mix and sell medicines

tonic liquid that people drink, like a medicine

World War I war fought in Europe from 1914 to 1918. The United States entered the war in 1917.

More Books to Read

An older reader can help you with these books:

Bell, Lonnie. *The Story of Coca-Cola*. Mankato, MN: Smart Apple Media, 2003.

Gould, William. *Coca-Cola: Makers of the World's Most Successful Product*. New York, NY: McGraw-Hill, 1996.

Index